Reminiscences of

Lafcadio Hearn

by
Setsuko Koizumi
(Mrs. Hearn)

Translated from the Japanese by
Paul Kiyoshi Hisada and Frederick Johnson

Zea Books
Lincoln, Nebraska
2022

ISBN 978-1-60962-227-5 paperback
ISBN 978-1-60962-228-2 ebook
doi:10.32873/unl.dc.zea.1314

Zea Books are published by the
University of Nebraska-Lincoln Libraries.

Electronic (pdf) edition available online at
https://digitalcommons.unl.edu/zeabook/

Print edition available from Lulu.com at
http://www.lulu.com/spotlight/unllib

University of Nebraska-Lincoln does not
discriminate based upon any protected status.
Please go to
http://www.unl.edu/equity/notice-nondiscrimination

INTRODUCTION

"When a ship sails away, she leaves smoke behind;
Alas, that smoke causes my heart to ache."

It is sad to be left behind. After spending years in a land which is not mine, amongst people whose language also is not mine, when I visit home, time knows no sympathy, and my two months pass away like an ever-fascinating dream. It was my last day in Japan, and in the morning I would sail away. I had seen everybody I wanted to meet, except one, Mrs. Setzuko Koizumi, who lives in Okubo, the outskirt district of Tokyo.

The pouring rain and long distance did not stop my going there. Not having her exact address might have discouraged me, but I felt it would make the visit still more interesting should I succeed.

Tokyo was an utterly strange city to me, and the development of the city had advanced with a Herculean stride. Taking one street car after another, transferring two or three times, I reached a station called Okubo, and inquired for the whereabouts of Mrs. Koizumi, but nobody seemed to know. I added the name Hearn, but even that brought no answer, until I said, "A Japanese woman who married a foreigner"; then they suggested the direction. After walking a distance of several . blocks, I came to a very artistic gate, which * led diagonally to a house, by a stone-paved walk, and there was the name Koizumi on the door.

Opening a sliding door of latticework, I said "Dozo —" (please —), and a young Japanese girl responded, who was one of Hearn's children. At my request to see the mistress of the house, she bowed politely, and returned with a young man, who was Kazuo, the eldest son of Hearn, who is in Waseda College. He resembles his father, but his color is typically Japanese. Telling him about my work of translation, and my admiration for his father, induced him to bring his mother to join in the conversation. I found her a woman of motherly appearance, and she showed in every way a fine Japanese character." One could tell easily that she was of Samurai descent.

When she observed my intense desire
to see Hearn's study, she guided me there,
where he worked until his last days, and
I found the place in order as neatly as he
left it. His desk was built up higher than
ordinary ones, on account of his eyesight,
and the row of books in the bookcase were
as if telling the stories of the days when
Hearn worked in this very room. In a cor-
ner of the study, I saw a modest Bud-
dhistic family altar, where was enclosed
a portrait photograph of Hearn, in front
of which rose the smoke of incense, like
a filmy gauze; and I naturally paid my
hearty homage to the spirit of the patri-
arch, the English writer who linked the
East and the West. There is no one who
did more to bring the inner thought and
ideal of Japan to the West than Hearn. He
received no public recognition, nor was he
decorated in Japan, but the outer world
places a crown of laurel upon him. "Todai
moto kurashi" (the foot of the beacon is
dark).

One of Hearn's three children, Kiyoshi,
who attends the art school, was out. Had
I met him I should have had the pleasure
of seeing all the Hearns. His name (which

means "unsophisticated," "cleanliness," or "good nature") is the same as mine; that interested me. "Please tell me why Sensei! named him Kiyoshi," I said. "Just because father liked the sound of the name," replied Kazuo.

While the two sticks of incense that I had offered burned serenely, my heart was filled with sentiment toward his work, and his words, often repeated in the classroom of the Tokyo Imperial College, "The pen is mightier than the sword." I bade them good-bye and thanked them for their courtesy, and was glad that I had seen the house and garden and flowers and trees on a rainy day, instead of a fine day. Meseems rainy days might be the days that Hearn enjoyed better than clear days with blue sky.

With the consent of Mrs. Hearn, I have translated her story into English, and first of all, I present a copy to be placed on the tomb of the deceased writer. May his spirit accept this copy, and may he think of the country that he adopted by choice, and his devoted wife, who has written her reminiscences of this gifted son of the Isle of Leucadia, Greece.

This little book came to be printed through the good efforts of my friend, Frederick Johnson. Without him, I never should have seen it in type. I share the name of translator with him, and I return to him full gratitude and thanks.

KIYOSHI HISADA

REMINISCENCES OF
LAFCADIO HEARN

I

HEARN came to Japan in the spring of the twenty-third year of Meiji (1891). He immediately discontinued his business relations with the publishing-house of Harper & Brothers. That is why he had great difficulty in earning a living after coming far away to a foreign land. He accepted a position in a school in Izumo, because Izumo was the oldest province where many shadows of great historic events would remain. He did not mind the isolation nor the inconveniences, and, as he was a bachelor, he did not care much about the salary. So he went there.

He stopped a night in Shimoichi, in Hoki Province, and there he saw a dance at the *Bon Matsuri* (Buddhist Festival of the Dead) which he thought very interesting. He crossed the lagoon from Yonago, and arrived in Matsué on the shore near a large bridge. It was the latter part of August. At that time the steam railway connected Tokyo with Okayama, but from that point he was obliged to cross mountain after mountain until he reached Yonago, and lodgings for the night were very poor.

Passing through a succession of villages, the traveler suddenly comes to Matsué, which is a very clean city, and one that surprises and astonishes the visitor. By crossing the large bridge, it is possible to obtain, toward the east, a distant view of Mount Oyama in Hoki Province, called "Izumo Fuji" by the natives because its shape resembles the other Fuji. The Ohashi River slowly flows in that direction. On the western horizon, sky and lake meet and mingle; square white sails appear to hover above the tranquil waters. Near the shore is an islet bearing five or six pine trees, and on it is a shrine to the goddess Benten. It seemed to me that this was Hearn's favorite view.

The population of Matsué was about forty thousand. It had been a feudal stronghold of Naomasa's, a relative by blood of Ieyasu, and, after several generations, became the home of a lord named Fumaiko. That is why there was a pronounced æsthetic atmosphere about this city in spite of its being in an isolated region. Hearn taught in the Middle School and in the Normal School. Mr. Nishida, dean of the professors, was unusually kind to him. They became very intimate, and liked each other well. Hearn had great confidence in Mr. Nishida, and always praised him. "Clever, kind, learned, and brave, he points out my mistakes; he tells me all; he is a real man, an amiable man, and not a flatterer." Mr. Nishida, unfortunately, was always suffering and never in good health. "He is always ill. How bad God is! I am angry," Hearn used to say. "This is a very cruel world that so good a man can be so ill. Why cannot the bad men have all the diseases?" Even after we came to Tokyo, Hearn worried about Mr. Nishida's health. Mr. Nishida died on the fifteenth of March, in the thirtieth year of Meiji. Once after his death, Hearn said: "To-day I thought that I saw Mr. Nishida. His back was toward me. I made my *kurumaya* hurry. It was astonishing how much that man resembled Mr. Nishida!" He felt very kindly toward the stranger because of that resemblance.

When he went to Waseda University, he thought that Professor Takada reminded him of Mr. Nishida, and he was exceedingly pleased.

At that time the governor was Mr. Kagoteda. He was very earnest about keeping alive the national spirit of former days. He had self-control, like a *daimyo* (feudal lord); he was fond of fencing, and was very skillful in that art. Just then there was a revival of the chivalry of *Bushido* (the practical religion of the old warrior class of feudal Japan), and its accompanying contests with swords and spears. Old-fashioned horse-races were held again, and old people of the past generation belonging to the *samurai* class could think that they were living once more in the days of their youth. Hearn was much delighted. He was invited to all those events, and was well received by the governor.

Everything he saw or heard was new to Hearn, and he took much pleasure in writing down whatever was interesting. The pupils and the teachers of the Middle School and of the Normal School all liked Hearn, and the local papers printed articles about him and praised him. He had this reputation: "Hearn is too good a man to be in so isolated a place."

But Hearn liked such isolated places. He liked Matsué far better than Tokyo. The island of Oki was superior to Nikko. He never saw Nikko. After coming to Matsué, he never had a chance to go there. He said he had no desire to see Nikko, although, if he had gone, I know that he would have liked that double row of *cryptomerias* (Japanese cedars) and the woods.

When I went to him, I found only one table and a chair, a few books, one suit of clothes, and one set of Japanese *kimono*.

When he returned from the school, he immediately put on a *kimono*, sat on a *zabuton* (square cushion for the floor), and smoked a pipeful of tobacco. He liked everything Japanese, and drew nearer and nearer to the Japanese style of living. Speaking of Western things, he said: "There are many beautiful things in Japan. Why do they imitate Western things?" That was his plaint. He always forgot himself when he saw an interesting or a beautiful object.

In Matsué he frequently went to banquets, and he often invited to his home and entertained there two or three teachers from the school. He enjoyed listening to the folklore and various popular songs. He liked Japanese costumes, and wore the *haori* and *hakama* (coat and wide plaited trousers for formal occasions) when he made the round of ceremonious calls at New Year's. He was received with old-fashioned ceremony at the governor's residence, and was exceedingly delighted with those occasions. When he first came to Matsué, he stopped for a while in a hotel on Zaimokucho, but soon hurried away to another place. There might have been other reasons, but the main cause of his departure was a little girl who suffered from a disease of the eyes. He thought of her with sorrow, and begged the little one's relatives to let her go to be treated at the hospital; but the landlord only said, "Yes, yes," and postponed doing so indefinitely. Hearn was angered, and left the hotel with the words, "Strange and unsympathetic man, who is without a parent's heart!" Then he moved to another place, and hired a *hanarézashiki* (detached dwelling in a garden). "However," said Hearn, "the girl is not in the least to

blame, only I am sorry for her." So he had
the doctor treat her and cure her.

He himself had weak eyes, and he always paid a great deal of attention to
them. When his first son was born, he
made a wish with great anxiety, saying,
"Come into this world with good eyes!"
He had always a deep sympathy for those
with poor eyes. At home, when Hearn saw
shosei-san (young students given homes in
private families) reading a newspaper or a
book on the floor, he would say to them at
once, "Hold up the book when you read!"

I married him a short time after he had
moved to his new quarters from the hotel.
Hearn had a peculiar temperament, and
it caused me much trouble. A man moved
into our neighborhood and called on him.
This man had been in the same hotel on
Zaimokucho, and was a friend of the hotel-keeper. He came to borrow a corkscrew.
After greeting him, Hearn asked, "Is it you
who stayed at that hotel in Zaimokucho,
and were a friend of the hotel-keeper's?"
The man answered, "Yes, I am his friend."
Hearn replied, "I dislike you because you
are that strange and unsympathetic fel-
low's friend. *Sayonara*. Good-bye!" and

left him and went inside the house. This man naturally did not understand what the trouble was, so I tried to explain, but I was very much embarrassed.

This *hanarézashiki* of Suetsugu commanded an excellent view of the lake, and the beautiful scene pleased Hearn immensely.

We began our married life there, but suffered from many inconveniences. Early in the summer of the twenty-fourth year of Meiji (1892), we moved over to a *samurai* estate and kept house. We moved with a maid and a pussy-cat. One evening in the early spring of that year while the air was yet chill and penetrating, I was standing on the veranda admiring the sunset on the lake, when I saw, directly below the veranda along the shore, four or five naughty children ducking pussy up and down in the water and cruelly teasing her. I begged pussy of the children, brought her back to the house, and told the story to Hearn. "Oh, poor puss!" he exclaimed. "What cruel children they were!" And he held the shivering pussy right in his bosom to warm her. That time I felt a great admiration for him.

After we moved to our estate, Kitabori, we missed the view of the lake, but we had left the noise of the city. There was a running stream directly in front of the gate, and on the other bank we could see the spire of the castle through the woods. This estate was different from others, being a *samurai* estate. We found it in very good taste, and the reception hall and all the rooms were well arranged. At the back were a hill and the garden, and this garden was a favorite spot where we enjoyed walking about in our *yukata* (light kimono for lounging), wearing garden clogs. The mountain pigeon coos, *"Te-te-pop, ka-ka-po-po !"* When he heard the mountain pigeon coo, Hearn used to call me to come to him. "Do you hear that? Isn't that delightful?" And he himself would imitate the sound, *"Te-te-pop, ka-ka-po-po!"* and ask, "Did I do it right?"

There was a lotus-pond in the garden, and we saw a snake in it. "Snakes never harm you unless you hurt them," Hearn said; and he shared his food from the table with the snake. "I am giving you this food so that you will not eat the frogs," he told the snake. Then he related some of the incidents in his life. "When I was in the West Indies, studying, the snakes would often crawl up my left arm, over my shoulders, and down my right arm. But I paid no attention to them and kept on studying. Snakes are not harmful; they are not bad."

It may seem funny for me to mention the fact that Hearn was an extremely honest man. He did not have the least evil in his mind. He had more delicate and kindly sentiments than a girl. During his childhood he had always been teased by malicious people until he cried. The keenness of his sensibility was astonishing.

We once took a trip in the Province of Hoki, to a place called Lake Togo. We wished to stay there for a week, but the inn was crowded with people having a gay time, drinking and making a great deal of noise. Hearn saw them, and immediately pulled my sleeve. "We cannot stay. This is *jigoku* (hell). It is no place for me, even for a second." In spite of the innkeeper's protests, and his greeting, *"Yoku irashai-mash'ta!* (Welcome!) This way, please!"* as he tried to lead the way, Hearn said, "I do not like it!" and left at once. Both the innkeeper and the *kurumaya* were

surprised. It was a very noisy and common
inn, and, naturally, I loathed the place,
but Hearn called it *jigoku*. He never had
the least patience with anything he disliked. I was still young then, and not used
to the world, so this peculiarity of Hearn's
caused me embarrassment many times.
This was Hearn's innate temperament,
and I thought it good.

As I remember, it was about this same
time that we visited the Kugurido near
Kaga-no-ura, in the Province of Izumo.
This place was a grotto on an island in
the sea, about two miles from the land.
Hearn was extremely fond of swimming,
and he swam all the way ahead of or behind the boat. He took great delight in
giving me an exhibition of the different
strokes used in swimming. When the boat
reached the cave, the noise of the waves
washing against the rocks made a fearful
sound, and the drops of water fell down
— *"potari! potari!"* The rowers knocked
against the side of the boat with a stone
— *"kong! kong!"* This was to notify the de-
mon that the boat was coming in. After
the noise of the rock — *"kong! kong!"* —
we heard a sound, *"chabong! chabong!"* as

if something had jumped into the water. The rowers began to tell many horrid stories, pathetic and tragic, about the spot.

Hearn was going to take off his clothes, which he had put on a little while before, but the rowers said, "Master, do not do so ! It is too dreadful to contemplate!" I also said, "Do not go in swimming in such a place! There are so many horrid fables about it that something frightful may dwell here."

But Hearn said, "The water is so beautiful, so dark a blue! The depth is unknown. It may be several million fathoms! It would be great fun!" He was very anxious to go in swimming, but finally renounced the idea. He was very sulky, and, even on the following day, he did not speak because of this disappointment. Several days later he said to me, "I once swam in a place where they said it was very dangerous, but I escaped without accident. Only I felt as if my body were melting away the minute I went in. I had a bad fever at once. Two of us went in at the same time. Suddenly my companion disappeared, and I noticed the tail of a big shark right in front of me."

Hearn was still young and very vigorous at the time when he lived in Matsué. He often recalled his West Indian days, and would say, "I wish I could show you the West Indies!"

In 1892, when it came the time for the summer vacation, Hearn went to visit the holy shrine of Kizuki. The day after his arrival, he wrote to me and asked me to come too. I went to the hotel, and found him absent; he was bathing in the sea. His money was in a stocking and scattered around — silver coins and banknotes were falling out. Hearn was so very careless with his money that it was almost amusing. He was born that way, and had no mind for so common a thing. Only when his children were born, or when he noticed that his body was becoming weak, did he take note of the state of his finances and begin to worry about his family.

The abbot of the shrine was a friend of Mr. Nishida's. He knew of Hearn's fondness for Japan, and he gave him an unusual reception. Hearn mentioned the fact that he was very desirous of seeing the Bon Festival dance. It was a little too early in the season, but the abbot gathered several hundred men just for that purpose, and they danced for us. Everybody who took part was delighted, and gladly did his best to show the movements of the dance. This dance was very gay, and Hearn said, "This is more like the harvest dance than the Bon Festival dance." During this trip he learned the "Kimigayo" (national anthem), and we used to sing it. Hearn was as innocent as a child in his pleasures.

After a fortnight we returned to Matsué, and, as it was about the time for the *Bon Odori* dance, we took a trip to Shimoichi in order to see the dances. We took no guide. Mr. Nishida had gone to Kyoto. It was our first journey of so long a distance as this one. When we reached Shimoichi, we made inquiry at the hotel where we had stopped on the way down the preceding year. "This year the police authorities have prohibited the dancing," the hotel proprietor told us. Hearn was much disappointed and felt very annoyed about it. "The police are worthless! The old customs of Japan, very interesting customs, are discarded. It is the Christians who are to blame; they cast aside all the Japanese ways, and try to imitate Western things," Hearn said, disgustedly.

On this occasion we hunted all around for the *Bon Odori* dances. We had the same trouble on this trip which we had had at the Togo hotel. At last we discovered a place where they were going to dance, but they received us insultingly, and threw sand at Hearn because he was a foreigner; they also refused to dance. Afterward they came to apologize. It was very strange. We returned to Matsué by the end of August, and we talked these things over with Mr. Nishida, who had come back from Kyoto, and enjoyed telling him what had happened while we were traveling about for a month. Besides this trip, we frequently went off and spent the night away from home.

Izumo was full of interest, and Hearn liked the place, but, after being used to living in a warm country like the West Indies, he suffered from the severe cold. At the school they only had one large *hibachi* (charcoal brazier) in the classroom. He complained of the cold to Mr. Nishida, who suggested that Hearn keep his overcoat on while giving lessons. At that time he had an overcoat that he used to wear in spite of the fact that he called it a seaman's. He had taste, but, as this example shows, he was very careless.

Let me recall the walks we had together in Kumamoto. One evening Hearn came in from a walk and said, "I will take you to a certain place to-morrow night. I have found a very interesting spot." It was not a moonlight night. We walked through lonely streets after leaving the house. When we reached the foot of a hill, he said, "It is on top of this." A narrow path led to the summit; shrubs and bamboos caught our feet, and we climbed to a graveyard. Under the dim starlight I saw a number of tombstones here and there, and I thought it very dismal. Then Hearn said, "Just listen to those frogs!" Again one evening, while in Kumamoto, he returned from his walk and remarked: "This evening I walked along a very lonely country road. I heard a dainty voice from out the darkness — it was you calling me. I stood still, but found nobody — nothing but darkness."

When Hearn was teaching in Kumamoto, we went to Oki Island from Hoki Province during the summer vacation time. We explored all the coves on that

island. We visited Saigo, Beppu, Ura-
no-go, and Hishiura. In the last place
we stopped for a week. Foreigners were
strange to the populace, and Hearn was
the first one who had ever come there.
There were mobs, and some of the crowd
filled the balcony of the house across the
street. Their weight broke the balcony, but
fortunately no one was injured. The police
were called out, and it was quite exciting.
In Saigo the chief physician of the hospital entertained us as Hearn was an unique
guest. He was much disturbed over our re-
cent experience, but, in order to make me
feel comfortable, he said, "It could n't have
been more amusing!" and pretended to be
very calm; but I understand that he wrote
in one of his books that he was much disturbed. We paid homage to the ancient emperor's mausoleum. We also visited Mount
Kuroki where Emperor Godaigo once lived.
Near this place at Beppu, I remember that
they had no cakes with the tea, and that
they offered us some roasted beans.

On our way home from Kizuki, we happened to see the *Bon* dance in the fishing
port of Sakai, in Hoki Province. Naturally,
all the participants were active fishermen,

and they clapped their hands vigorously and were very lively in their movements. Hearn remarked that it was the liveliest dance he had ever witnessed. The dance in Kizuki was merry and cheerful, like the harvest dance; the dance in Shimoichi offered veneration to the souls of the departed; and the dance in Sakai was overflowing with enthusiasm and animation.

I always remember a place in the mountains where we stayed when we were crossing from Hoki Province into Bingo Province. The inn was a very wretched one, but Hearn liked it. The *kurumaya* had agreed to go about six miles farther on, but, because of delays and broken roads, the sun set before we crossed the mountains and it grew dark. We traveled over the mountain in the gathering gloom. It was nearly autumn, and we heard the noises of all kinds of insects as if the whole mountain were alive with the songs of insects, and yet this murmur only emphasized the tranquillity of the spot. "Is n't there an inn near here?" asked Hearn. "Yes, a little way beyond, there are seven houses. One of them takes lodgers, and I wish you would stop there," answered the *kurumaya*, apologetically. As I remember, it was about ten o'clock when we reached the inn. It was really a small, shabby farmhouse with a queer atmosphere about it. The *andon* (paper lantern) gave a very poor light, and the proprietors were an old man and his wife. We saw three bravo-like men talking there. We were shown to a room upstairs, and the old woman left us a tiny lamp and never came up again.

It was right after the floods of 1893, and we heard the torrent rushing down the near-by river-bed. The noise of the water — "Go ... go" — made a terrific sound.

Now and then the room was lighted by fireflies which flew into and out of the house; there were great numbers of them. While we were looking out of the window, we felt some kind of insect come swarming around us as if something were thrown over us on our hands and faces. They were very nasty insects. Sometimes crickets came and sang close beside us as we knelt on the floor.

We occasionally heard the bravo-like men talking, and the stairs would creak from time to time. We thought that the bravos were climbing up, and we could not help thinking of tales of the olden days which we had read in books of adventure. The old woman brought us our dinners on trays. I asked her what those insects were, and she told us that they were called *Natsu-mushi* (summer insects), and that there was nothing unusual about them. It was indeed an isolated spot, and we felt as if we were living in a dream. Hearn said, "This is an interesting place, and I should like to pass another night here." Those hotels for foreigners with modern facilities in Hakone and elsewhere were not to Hearn's liking, but this kind of inn fascinated him. If I had agreed, we might have stayed there much longer in the Province of Hoki, where the storm was heavy on the sea. Hearn always wished to take a trip through the Province of Hida, but he never had the opportunity to do so.

When we were returning from Kobé, Hearn said that he could not stay in Tokyo for more than three years. From the very first he never cared for Tokyo, and compared the city to *"jigoku"* (hell). I was eagerly looking forward to seeing Tokyo, but Hearn said to me, "You are thinking that Tokyo still resembles that Yedo which

Hiroshigé depicted with his brush and colors." One of our reasons for going to Tokyo
was to give me an opportunity to see the
city. Hearn often said, "The three years
have passed, and now you have finished
your sightseeing in Tokyo. Let us go back!"

II

On August 27, 1897, we went to Tokyo from Kobé. We heard at first that there were houses assigned to professors of the university, but we wished to live far from the university, in the suburb, and, although we hunted for a house, we could not find a good one.

We received word that there was a good, spacious house in the district of Ushigomé, if I remember rightly. We went to see it, and found that it was one story in height, and built in the old style. I imagine that it had originally been erected for *hatamoto* (a commander of the *shogun's* camp) or *daimyo*. The gateway looked like the gateway to a temple, and, after entering, we found that the house looked more and more like a temple. It had a large garden, with a good-sized lotus-pond. But, once inside, we noticed something very ghostly about the place, and felt strange. Hearn liked it, and said, "This is a very interesting house." He thought of taking it, but I could not bear to live in such a place. I learned afterward that it was haunted, and that ogres had dwelt in it. On that account the rental grew less and less, and finally it was torn down. When I told this to Hearn, he said, "Why did we not go there to live? I was sure that it was an interesting house!"

We moved to Tomihisa-cho. Here the garden was small, but the view was excellent. Hearn was particularly fond of this place. The neighboring building was a Buddhist temple called Kobudera. This temple had once been called Hagidera, and there was an abundance of *hagi* (bush-clover) growing in the grounds. The temple was very weatherworn, but it possessed a grove of great cedar trees where an atmosphere of tranquillity always reigned. Every day we visited this temple in the morning and the evening. We soon made friends with the abbot, and he used to tell us interesting stories of Buddhist lore. That is why I often went there too.

Hearn went about in a *kimono*, feeling proud and cheerful. When any of his intimate friends came to call, he took them to that interesting temple of Kobudera. And the children always thought that papa was at the temple, if he was not to be seen in the house.

Many times while out walking, he said, "Mamma-san, is it hard to get in a temple? Is n't there any way by which I could live in the temple?"

I replied, "You are not a priest, so perhaps you cannot very well do so."

"I should prefer to be a priest," Hearn said; "and how pleased I should be if I could be one."

"If you should become a priest, how funny you would look with your large eyes and high nose — a fine priest!" I remarked.

"You could become a nun at the same time, and Kazuo [our eldest son] a novice. How cute he would look! Every day we should read the scriptures and take care of the graves. That would be true happiness !"

"Pray that you may be born a priest in the next world!"

"That is my wish," replied Hearn.

One day, as usual, we took a walk to the neighboring temple. Suddenly Hearn exclaimed, "Oh! oh!" I did not know what had happened, and was frightened. Then I saw that three large cedar trees had been cut down, and Hearn was gazing at them. "Why did they cut down those trees?"

"This temple must be very poor, and they must need some money," I replied.

"Why did n't they tell me about it? I can easily give a little money to help them. I should have been happier to have given them some money and saved the trees. Think how long a time was necessary for those trees to grow from little sprouting seeds!" He was very down-hearted. "I begin to dislike that abbot. I am sorry for him because he has no money, but I am more sorry for those trees, Mamma-san!"

Hearn came out of the temple gate in a lifeless manner, as if some great event had taken place. He sat down in the chair in his study, and was very much depressed. "It hurts my heart to see that sight," he said. "There will be no more joy to-day. Please beg the abbot not to cut down any more trees." After that time he seldom visited the temple.

The old abbot soon went away, and a new young abbot succeeded him. Then all the trees were cut down. When we moved away, there were no trees to be seen, the graves were gone, new tenements had been built, and the whole place changed. What Hearn had called his world of tranquillity vanished in that manner. Those three fallen trees had been the beginning of the end.

I had always wished to live in a house of small size, — a quiet country place with a large garden and many trees. After the profanation of Kobudera I looked about in many directions. There was a house for sale in Nishi Okubo. This house was purely Japanese, and there was not a building in foreign style to be seen in the neighborhood.

I always desired a house of my own, even if a small one, in preference to a rented house, and I wished to build one. When I suggested this, Hearn said, "Have you money?" and I answered, "Yes, I have." Then he said, "Great fun! I will build a house in the island of Oki"; and when I opposed that, he added, "We will build one in Izumo Province." We even went in search of land, but I did not like Izumo well enough to build there, and we finally decided to buy this estate and to build additions later.

Hearn always wished to live in the midst of purely Japanese surroundings, and he went to inspect the house himself.

It was on the outskirts of the town and had a bamboo grove back of it, and it pleased him very much. In adding to the house, he wished to have a room where he could light a stove during the severe cold of the winter, and he also wished to have his desk face the west. He had no other request, but everything must be in Japanese style; excepting this, he made no suggestions. If ever I happened to consult him, he would say, "Well, you do as you please. I know how to write, that is all, and you, Mamma-san, know much better." He would pay no more attention, and if I insisted, he would add, "I have no time"; and he left the entire affair to me.

"When that house is all ready, you might say, 'Papa-san, please come to our new house in Okubo to-day.' Then I will say good-bye to this house, and will go to Okubo just as I would go to the university. That is all." I actually did as he requested. He disliked to lose time. We moved to Nishi Okubo on the nineteenth day of the third month, in the 35th year of Meiji (1903). Everything was made in Japanese style. Hearn was very fond of Japanese sliding paper doors. The only Western feature was

the glass doors in the room where he had
the stove. Hearn greatly enjoyed the day
on which we moved. As I was helping him
arrange his books on the shelves, he said,
"How delightful this is!" This house was
larger than the one in Tomihisa-cho, and
at that time Okubo was more rural than
it is now; it was extremely quiet, and we
heard the nightingales singing in the bamboo grove at the back of the house. Hearn
continued, "It hurts my heart." I asked,
"Why?" He replied, "It is too pleasant to
last. I pray that we may live here a long
time. But what do you think?"

Hearn avoided all complex society.
Sometimes when a distinguished person paid a call, he would tell the maid to
say that he had no time, and wished to
be excused. It was always embarrassing
for *shosei-san* and the maids when callers
came to the door. Hearn was so method-
ical a man that he did not wish to meet
any one or make a call that would inter-
rupt his study.

I used to brush out the rooms about
twice every day. It was a diversion for me,
but Hearn said, "You have a mania for
cleaning." He hated the noise of cleaning.

I always cleaned the house while he was at the university, or when, he was at home, I cleaned it before he got up and had his breakfast. Otherwise, if I asked him to let me clean, he made me promise to do it in five or six minutes. During that time he walked around the *roka* (corridor) or in the garden.

Hearn avoided society and seemed eccentric because he valued so highly things of beauty and of interest and was fond of them. For that same reason I frequently observed that he wept when alone by himself, and he was irritated or elated in an abnormal degree. His greatest pleasure was to live and write in the world of his imagination. That is why he was a recluse and was chary of his time.

"Won't you do something else for pleasure besides writing in your own study?" I would ask him.

"You know very well that my only diversion is to think and to write. If I have anything to write, I never get tired. When I write I forget everything. Please tell me some stories," he would reply.

I would say, "I have told you all; I have none to tell."

"Therefore you should go out and see or hear something interesting, and come back and tell me all about it. It will never do for you just to stay at home."

He wrote with great eagerness, and it disturbed his work if there was the least noise of opening and shutting doors, walking in the corridor, and if the children became unduly excited. Anything of that nature worried me, and I tried to prevent those noises from reaching Hearn's ears. When I wished to enter his study, I chose the time when he was singing or hitting the bowl of his pipe against the *hibachi* to empty it. At other times he would not answer, for an interruption or the least noise irritated him greatly. That was the general atmosphere of the entire house.

After we moved to Okubo, the house was much more spacious and the study was far from the front door and the children's room, so we made it a world of tranquillity without a single noise. Even then he complained that I broke his train of thought by opening the bureau drawers, so I made every effort to open the drawers more quietly. On such occasions I always remembered not to break his beautiful soap-bubble (not to destroy his day-dreams). That is how I thought about it, so I never felt provoked when he scolded me.

While working on his manuscripts he frequently made unusual inquiries, and I often wished, because I was anxious, that he would not work so hard. When we were in Matsué I was still young, and I thought that Hearn was losing his mind. I worried about it, and asked Mr. Nishida's opinion, and found out that he was too deeply interested in his work. Hearn was extremely fond of ghost stories, and he used to say, "Books of ghost stories are my treasures." I hunted for them from one second-hand bookstore to another.

On quiet nights, after lowering the wick of the lamp, I would begin to tell ghost stories. Hearn would ask questions with bated breath, and would listen to my tales with a terrified air. I naturally emphasized the exciting parts of the stories when I saw him so moved. At those times our house seemed as if it were haunted. I often had horrid dreams and nightmares. Hearn would say, "We will stop talking about such things for a while"; and we would do so. He was pleased when I told a story he liked.

When I told him the old tales, I always first gave the plot roughly; and wherever he found an interesting place, he made a note of it. Then he would ask me to give the details, and often to repeat them. If I told him the story by reading it from a book, he would say, "There is no use of your reading it from the book. I prefer your own words and phrases — all from your own thought. Otherwise, it won't do." Therefore I had to assimilate the story before telling it. That made me dream. He would become so eager when I reached an interesting point of a story! His facial expression would change and his eyes would burn intensely. This change was extraordinary. For example, take the story "O Katsu San of Yurei-daké," in the first part of the book, "Kotto." As I was narrating that story, his face became extremely pale and his eyes fixed. That was not unusual, but this once I suddenly felt afraid. He sighed one long breath, and said, "Very interesting!" when I finished it.

He asked me to say, "Alas! blood!" and repeat it several times. He inquired how it had probably been said, and in what tone of voice; what kind of night it was, and how the wooden clogs would sound. "I think it was in this way," he would say; "how do you think, yourself?" and so forth, — all of this was not at all in the book, — and he would consult with me about it. Had any one seen us from the outside, we must have appeared like two mad people.

The story of "Yoshi-ichi" in the first part of "Kwaidan" pleased Hearn exceedingly. He made that story from a very short one, with great effort and determination. He wished to make one part of it sound stronger. He thought that *"Mon o aké"* (Open the door) was not an emphatic enough expression for a *samurai*, and he made it *"Kaimon"* (This latter word means "Open the door," like the former, but would be more fitting in the speaker's mouth.)

While we were working on this story of "Miminashi-Yoshi-ichi," night fell, but we lighted no lamp. I went into the adjoining room, and called out in a small voice, "Yoshi-ichi! Yoshi-ichi!"

"Yes," Hearn answered, playing the part, "I am blind. Who are you?" and remained silent. In this way he worked and became absorbed in it.

One day at that time, when I came home from a walk, I brought a *miyagé* (gift) of a little clay figure, a blind musician playing a *biwa* (a native four-stringed lute), and, without saying a word, I left it on his desk. Hearn, as soon as he noticed it, was delighted, and exclaimed, "Oh! Yoshi-ichi!" as if he saw some one whom he was expecting to meet. And sometimes when he heard during the night the swish of the bamboo leaves in the wind near his study, he would say, "Ah! there goes a Heiké!" And when he heard the wind, he listened to it earnestly, and said, "That is the waves of the Dan-no-ura!" — "A spot on the coast near Shimonoseki where the great *Taira* or *Heiké* Clan was exterminated April 25, 1185, by the rival *Minamoto* or *Genji* Clan led by the intrepid Yoshitsune." (Terry's *Japanese Empire*.)

Perhaps I might ask him, "Have you written that story?" He would reply, "That story has no brother. I shall still wait for a while. Perhaps I may see a good brother coming. I might leave it in a drawer for seven years, and even then I might come across a good brother." This is an example of how long it sometimes took him to write one story.

We both knew the heroine of the "Diary of a Woman" in "Kotto," and we kept the secret and never mentioned her name, but we often took an offering of incense and flowers to her grave.

While writing "Tanabata" Hearn wept, and I wept also, and thus we completed that book.

While writing "Ghostly Japan" Hearn worked very hard. "This book will kill me," he said. "It is no easy matter to write so large a volume in so short a time; there is no one to help me, and I think it very trying to accomplish such a task." This work was done after his dismissal from the university. He felt very hard and provoked because of his dismissal, and thought that he had been treated very indifferently. Things which were of ordinary occurrence Hearn accepted in a very sensitive manner.

He never had any desire to give his services to the university for a long time. "If it is necessary to spend such long hours in the university, there will be no time left for writing," was his usual complaint, and it was n't the dismissal that troubled him, but the way in which they treated him.

When the manuscript (of "Ghostly Japan") was finished, he was greatly pleased, and had it wrapped very tightly (he was very proud of doing up the manuscript securely — sometimes he put in a piece of board, and made it as heavy as a stone). He wrote the address neatly, and sent the manuscript by registered mail. He received a cablegram, saying "Good," and two or three days later he was dead. He looked forward eagerly to the publication of this book. A little while before his death, he said, "I can hear the noise of the tick-tack of setting the type for 'Ghostly Japan.'" He was anxious to see it published, but he passed away without that gratification, and it makes me sad, even now, to think about it.

When he took a pen to write, he kept his eyes near the paper and began with great energy. At such times you might call him, but it would bring no answer, and he would not move for anything. He was of a very nervous temperament, but frequently I found him quite oblivious to his surroundings.

One night about eleven o'clock I opened the *shoji* (sliding paper window) and smelt dense smoke from the oil lamp. To my astonishment I found that the wick of the lamp was way up and that the room was dark with smoke. Hearn was almost suffocating, but he was writing so enthusiastically that he noticed nothing, although he had a very sensitive nose for odors. I hurriedly opened the *shoji* and let in the air, and said, "Papa-san! how dangerous it was that you did not know the lamp was on fire!" He exclaimed, "Why was I so stupid!"

III

It was our custom for the three children to go upstairs and shout, "Papa, come down; supper is ready!" Hearn always replied, "All right, sweet boys!" and looked so delighted, sometimes almost dancing about. But there were occasions when he was working so hard that even the children's announcement would not bring any response, and they could get no answer, "All right!" At such times we might wait and wait, but he would not appear in the dining-room. Then I would go up myself, and say, "Papa-san, we have been waiting a long time, and all the things will taste bad. I wish you would hurry up. All the children are waiting." Then Hearn would ask, "What is it?" I would reply, "What's the matter with you? This will never do; it is dinner-time. Won't you take some dinner?" "I? Have n't I had dinner yet? I thought I had finished it. That's funny!"

That is the way it would be, and I would continue, "You had better wake up from your dream! The tiny children will cry." Hearn would reply, "*Gomen nasai!* Pardon me!" and follow me to the dining-room. On such occasions he was funny or absent-minded; he would forget to divide the bread with the children, and would say, "No," and begin to eat fast. If the children asked for bread, he would come to himself and say, "Pardon! pardon! did n't I give you any?" and begin to cut the bread. While cutting it, he would lose himself again, and eat the piece himself.

Before meals he took a little whiskey, but later wine was suggested on account of his health. When absent-minded he often mistook the whiskey for the wine and poured it into a glass to drink, or put salt in his coffee; and when the children drew his attention to it he would say, "Really! Is n't Papa stupid!" and become lost in thought again. Often I had to say to him, "Papa-san, it is about time that I should ask you to wake up from your dream!"

He had no particular preference nor dislike for any dish. Of the Japanese food, he liked the pickles and *sashimi* (raw fish) or anything else. He began his meal with the side-dishes and finished it with one bowl of rice, and of *seiyo-ryori* (foreign food); he was fond of plum-pudding and a thick cut of beefsteak. He especially enjoyed smoking. During dinner he would talk on different topics. I would tell him about the news in the Japanese papers, and he would reciprocate with the news in the Western papers. The newspapers which we took for a long time were the "Yomiuri" and the "Asahi." While we were eating, tiny Kiyoshi might peep through the *shoji*. The cat and the dog would come beneath the window. Each one would share his food with them, and they would eat very eagerly. When we had finished dining, we all sang songs together.

Often I found Hearn very much elated or very sad. Sometimes he would walk the corridor almost as if he were dancing, and laughing to himself. When I heard him, I would ask, "Papa-san, is there anything amusing?" Then he would burst out laughing, and laugh until the tears came into his eyes. This was when he happened to recall something funny in the paper, or something amusing that I had told him.

In the same way he would fall into deep thought, or become absorbed in ghost stories. Such moods might make one think that he would n't tell a joke, but he frequently told very refined jokes. Some one said to me that he never met the *sensei* (professor) when he did not tell a joke. When things were amusing, the whole world appeared amusing, and when he was sad, it seemed to him that the whole world was sad. While telling ghost stories he would transport himself into that world, or become the hero of the story. If he felt deeply a story he was hearing, his face and the color of his eyes would change. He would say "Such and such a world," and used the word *world* often.

Hearn's habitual voice was dainty, like a woman's, and his way of laughing was also very feminine; but sometimes he would become very energetic and excited in a dainty (*sic*) talk and would express himself very powerfully. He had two ways of laughing. One was dainty, and the other was uproarious, disregardful of everything. This laughter made the whole family laugh, and it was so amusing that even the maid could n't help laughing. At the time of Hearn's dismissal from the university, Mr. MacDonald, who was then stationed in Japan, came every Sunday from Yokohama to see him. We often heard that uproarious laughter of

Hearn's from the study, and the whole family laughed too.

There used to be a conch-shell on a table in the study. I brought it back as a miyagé, because it was so large, one time when I went to Enoshima with the children. Hearn blew into the shell, and it made a big noise. He was pleased, saying, "It sounds so well because I have strong lungs. What a funny noise!" he added, puffing out his cheeks. We came to an agreement. Every time he wished a charcoal fire for lighting his pipe, he was to blow this conch-shell. When he found no fire, he would blow and make a big noise that would vibrate in sound-waves, like "po-wo." Then it was heard even in the kitchen. We would keep the house so quiet, not making the least noise, and then would come the roar of the conch-shell. Particularly in the evening it sounded extraordinary. I took special care to have a charcoal fire always ready for him, but he wished to blow the shell; so the minute he saw that the charcoal was gone, he blew delightedly. It must have been fun for him. Often we were bringing the fire, and were already near his study, when we heard him blowing. The maid used to say, laughing, "There goes the shell!"

When Hearn saw anything well done, he appreciated it sympathetically.

We often enjoyed going to the exhibitions of paintings in Ueno Park. Hearn paid no attention to the painters' names. When he liked a picture, he paid the price no matter how dear it was, and would say, "Very reasonable! very reasonable!" "How do you like that picture? " he would ask me. I might reply, "The price is too dear." I would give this answer because he liked to buy without paying any attention to the expense. Then he would say, "No, I'm not speaking about the price, I'm speaking about the picture. Do you think it good?" And if I answered in the affirmative, Hearn would continue, "If you think so, we will buy it. I think that this price is very reasonable. We ought to pay a little more for it." If the painting was worth while, he always wished to give more than the set price, and would ask them to hurry to stick on the ticket "sold."

When both of us were sight-seeing in Kyoto we went to such places as the temple Chion-in, the Ginkakuji, and the

Kinkakuji. At those places they had a fixed price of five or ten sen admission fee, and when Hearn liked the place he would offer fifty sen or one yen (fifty cents), and if I suggested to him that it was unnecessary and rather embarrassing, he would n't listen to me and would say, "No, no, I should be ashamed otherwise." It seemed very queer to the people in the temples, and they would ask for his name, but naturally we did not give it.

When we were in Matsué, we took a walk one day to a near-by temple. Here we saw a small, stone statue of the Buddhist divinity Jizo that interested us. We wished to know who had executed it, and, by inquiring at the temple, we discovered that the name of the sculptor was Arakawa. This man had good talent, although he had the reputation of being very eccentric. He had had no education, and was not ambitious. Though suffering from poverty, this old man could not finish a work for any one in a given time, and it usually took him two or three years to do each piece. Hearn thought that he was interesting, and made him a present of three large casks of *sake* (liquor made from rice).

Later we invited him to our home and gave him dinner; Hearn also went to call on him in his own untidy house. Hearn ordered a piece of sculpture, and paid him more than he would accept willingly. There is a piece of sculpture in our house which is by Arakawa, the statue of the Emperor Tenchi, and though it was not a particularly good piece of work, Hearn bought it from a sense of admiration for this "poor genius."

One summer Hearn and I went to a dry-goods store to buy two or three *yukata*. The salesman showed us a large variety. That pleased Hearn immensely. He bought this one and that one, while I kept protesting, saying, "There is no need of buying so many." Finally, he bought about thirty pieces, and astonished the clerks in the shop by saying, "But, you see, these are only one and a half or two yen. I do so wish you to wear different kinds of *yukata*. Only to see them on you will give me great pleasure." That is the way in which he would act when he liked anything.

He was not very keen about the Japanese who wore European costumes. It annoyed him especially to see the women in Western fashions and speaking English.

Once we went to a bazaar in Ueno Park. Hearn, pointing to an article, inquired its cost very quietly in Japanese of a saleswoman, who answered him in English. Hearn was disgusted; he pulled my sleeve and walked away without making any purchase.

After he accepted the position in Waseda University, he was invited to Professor Takada's house. Mrs. Takada came to meet him at the door, and said, *"Yoku oidé kudasai mash'ta"* (Welcome), and showed the way. Instead of using English, she spoke in elegant Japanese. That pleased Hearn so much that he told me about it as soon as he came back.

While reading a local newspaper, I noticed an article about an aged peer who loathed Western fashions and liked everything Japanese. The maids in his house had the *obi* (girdle) tied in just such a way, the coiffure arranged in just such a way, and the *kimono* long and flowing in the most old-fashioned way, as at court. There were no modern lamps in the house, but old-fashioned paper lanterns; no soap and no Western innovations. Even the daily newspaper was excluded, and the old-fashioned customs were observed by the household servants. On that account no one cared to enter his employ, and would say, *"Mappira gomen"* (I beg to be entirely excused).

When I read that account to Hearn, he said, "How interesting it is!" and he was greatly delighted. "I simply adore a person like that; he would be one of my best friends. I am consumed with desire to see that house. I have nothing Western about me."

To this I replied, "You may have nothing Western about you, but look at your nose!"

And he said, "Oh! what can I do with my nose? Pity me because of this, for I, Koizumi Yakumo, truly love Japan more than any Japanese."

We had the children wear white *tabi* (socks). Hearn liked white ones better than black ones, and thought it was so nice to see the Japanese showing their white tabi beneath their *kimono*.

Hearn preferred to have the children wear *geta* (wooden clogs) than shoes. He pointed to his own toes: "Look at them! I don't wish my children's toes to become like that."

He did not like anything in extreme style. He cared very little about having his *kimono* well creased. He was not very fastidious. He cared for neither a swallow-tailed nor a Prince Albert coat. He always said of them, and of white shirts and silk hats, — "How barbarous they are!"

When we came from Kobé to Tokyo, he had a Prince Albert coat made for the first time at my request. I said, "You must have a Prince Albert because you are an university professor." He replied, "No; I told Professor Toyama that I dislike formal dress. I will not appear on an occasion where I have to wear it. Professor Toyama agreed with me that it would be all right. A Prince Albert coat would never do."

He had one made at last, but he wore it only four or five times. Whenever he had to wear it he always made a fuss. He would put it on unwillingly, saying, "I simply wear this to please you. Whenever I go out, you always wish me to put on a new suit or a Prince Albert, all of which I hate. This is no joke; I mean it." I knew that he did not like it, but I regretfully made him do so. He thought that it was my fault that he had to wear them.

Once I said to him jokingly, "Here are your Prince Albert and silk hat. You must wear them, for His Majesty has granted you an audience because you have written so much and so well about Japan." He replied, *"Mappira gomen"* the phrase he had learned awhile before when listening to the article in the paper about the aged peer. He liked the sound of the word *"Mappira"* and used it often.

He always wore a sack suit when he went out, but preferred a *kimono* or *yukata*. He never carried a cane nor an umbrella. It might rain, but he came home unconscious of it unless it was a torrent. Then, perhaps, he would take a *kuruma* (jinrikisha). He wore army boots, and was not concerned about the fashions. "A Japanese laborer's feet are much handsomer than those of a Westerner." I think that he always liked Japan better than the West, and a dream-world better than this world of reality. He did not fail to say, "Pleasant dreams," before retiring. He was exceedingly pleased to hear tales about my dreams.

It seems that it was his custom to wear neither white nor colored shirts. When he had to wear one with a Prince Albert, he wore a collar that was very low. He had fine taste in everything, but paid very little attention to his apparel, and he did not trouble to be particular, although he always wore excellent shirts and hats. He went all the way to Yokohama for his shirts, and ordered one dozen each time. The hats that he bought were felt, had a wide brim, and he chose the best.

He disliked superficial beauty, and paid no attention to what was in vogue; he hated anything modern, and loathed pretentious kindness. He did not believe in false teeth or artificial eyes. "They are all false," he would say; and disliked them all. He hated the Christian missionaries as he found many dishonest people among them; but he owned three Bibles, and told his eldest son that that was the book he must read a great deal.

Of the Japanese fairy tales, he liked Urashima Taro the best. When he simply heard the name Urashima, he exclaimed aloud with joy. saying, "Ah! Urashima!" He often stood in the corridor and hummed the tune, *"Haru no hino kasumeru sora ni, suminoé no . . . !"* (" Misty spring days

in a far-off land . . . ! ") He remembered
it well. Even I learned it by heart by listening to him. At the exhibition of paintings in Ueno Park, he bought the picture
of Urashima as soon as he saw it without
asking the price.

He liked hot weather best, and therefore enjoyed summer more than the other
seasons. He preferred a western aspect.
His study was built facing the west. He
took great pleasure in the sunsets. Whenever he saw the sun setting, he called me
and the children. We would hurry to him,
and even then he often said, "You are minutes too late. The sunset has begun to be
poor. How disappointed I am for you!" He
would sing, *"Yu-yaké, koyaké, asu tenki ni
naré"* (Great sunset, little sunset, may to-
morrow be good weather), and would make
the children sing too. When we went to
Yakizu, he played on the beach with the
children and with Otokichi, the *"Hiraita,
hiraita, nanno hana ga hiraita? Renge
no hana hiraita . . ."* (Open, open! what
flower opened? The lotus-flower opened!)
He played with the children very guile-
lessly (*sic*). He used to sing, and join in
the chorus with the children, that song

called "Has Commander Hirosé died ? " He would come out quietly to the room where the children were playing and singing and sing the songs with them. Some time ago the Mitsukoshi store sold cigarette cases made from the timber that had been used in the S.S. Fukui Maru. (Commander Hirosé was the idolized hero of Port Arthur, and the Fukui Maru was the steamer sunk by him to blockade the harbor channel of Port Arthur.) On that very day Hearn sang unexpectedly about Commander Hirosé, so I thought it a coincidence and kept the song in the case.

He was interested in "Hokku" (poems of short stanzas) and remembered many of them. He put tunes to these poems, and sang them while talking in the corridor. Sometimes he himself composed, and attributed his compositions to Basho [1] by way of jest.

We had an opportunity to see wrestling-matches in Matsué. Tani-no-oto, the *ozeki* (champion) was there. Hearn thought that Japanese wrestling was more interesting than the Western form of the

[1] Basho, famous poet.

sport. He often recalled the name of the
champion, and used the name Tani-no-oto
to describe anything fat.

Hearn told me that he used to go to the
theater every day while he was working
as a newspaper reporter in America. He
knew all the famous actors and had associated with them as a friend; he had also
frequented the dressing-rooms and stud-
ied the theaters. In Japan, he only went
to the theater twice, once in Matsué and
once in Kyoto. He told me that it caused
him suffering to sit among the audience in
a theater for many hours; but he always
wished to have his children see the plays
by good actors, and often urged me to go
to see them. He asked me not to fail to see
the plays by Danjuro. When I came back
from those plays, I would have to tell him
all about the stage, the audience, and all
the details. He would listen most atten-
tively and delightedly. He wished to meet
Danjuro and ask him questions regard-
ing the theater, but Danjuro died before
Hearn had that opportunity. Hearn often remarked, before his own death, that
he wished to study the Japanese plays.
Once he asked me to look up information

concerning the play *"Sanjusan-gen-do"* (translated under the title of "The Willow Tree"). After that, he frequently told me that he was going to begin his autobiography. There were a few parts done, but any writing concerning the theater was not finished before his death.

I often recall memories of morning-glories. When the end of autumn drew near, and the green leaves were beginning to turn yellow, there was always the last morning-glory of the season blossoming so lonesomely by itself. When Hearn saw that lonely flower, he admired it. "Will you please look at it? What beautiful courage and what honest sentiment! Please give it a word of praise. That dainty flower still blooms until the end. Just give it a word of praise!"

That morning the morning-glory ceased to bloom. My mother thoughtlessly pulled off the blossom and threw it away. The following morning Hearn went over to the fence and was greatly disappointed. He said, "Grandma's a fine woman, but she performed a sorry deed to the morning-glory."

One of the children made finger-marks on a new *fusuma* (sliding door) with his small, untidy hand. Hearn said, "My child spoiled that beauty!" He always felt keenly against mutilating or damaging beauty of any kind. He used to teach the children that even a picture you could buy for half a penny would be valuable if it was kept a long time.

Hearn used to tell me to be suspicious of people. He was exceedingly honest, and was easily fooled; he knew this himself, and that is why he used to talk as he did. He was a very critical man. For instance, when he was doing business with publishers in foreign countries, and because he was so far away, the publisher would take the liberty of deciding the arrangement of such things as book-covers and illustrations without consulting Hearn, who was very particular about all details. At such times Hearn was often made furiously angry. When he received a letter from the publishing-house, he would immediately write back a fierce (*sic*) answer in anger, and order it to be mailed at once; but then I would say "Yes," and hold it over a mail. Two or three days afterward, when he had become calm, he would regret that he had written too severely, and would ask,

"Mamma-san, have you mailed that letter?" I would answer, "Yes," and watch to
see whether he really regretted it. If so, I
would give him the letter. He would be immensely pleased, and say, "Mamma-san,
you are the only one!" and would begin a
new letter in a milder tone.

Hearn preferred women of quiet dispo-
sition to those of lively temperament. He
liked bashful, downcast eyes better than
those of Westerners. He liked the eyes of
Kwannon and Jizo (Buddhist divinities).
When we were having our pictures taken,
he always told us to look downward, and
he himself had his picture taken in that
attitude.

Just before our eldest boy came, he
thought that children were lovely, and borrowed one and kept it in our house.

At the time of our eldest son's birth he
was very pleased, although extremely anxious. He hoped that my delivery would be
easy, and felt sorry for my suffering. And
he said, "On such an occasion I ought to be
studying," and he went out to the *hanarézashiki* and worked.

When he heard the new-born baby's
first cry, he was affected by a very queer

feeling a feeling that he had never experi-
enced in all his life. When he saw the baby
the first time, he could find no words, and
later told me that he had had no breath,
and he often spoke of it in retrospect. He
loved the baby very much.

The following year he went to Yokohama alone (his only other trip by himself had been once to Nagasaki, where he
had intended to stay for a week; but he
came back after one night, saying, "Never
again!"), and returned with a great many
toys. We were all surprised when we saw
so many, and among them we found some
for which he had paid five and ten *yen*.

Hearn was an early riser. All the year
round, including New Year's morning,
he gave a lesson to our eldest son for one
hour. When he was teaching at the university, he had to be there at eight o'clock on
Tuesdays, so on that day the lesson was
given in the afternoon. It took one hour
to go to the university and back. During
the daytime, he used to go out for a two
hours' walk about two or three o'clock,
and sometimes he read and wrote letters
or prepared his lectures; he used to do his
literary work chiefly at night. At night, he

generally worked until twelve, and I often found him writing when he was unable to sleep.

When our daughter Suzuko came, he felt that, in his old age, he would be unable to foresee the girl's future, and he said, "What pain is in my heart!" He worried over it with more sorrow than rejoicing.

When I wished to go out, I made it my rule to go out on Thursdays, when he had more hours of lessons at the university. On the previous day he would kindly advise me to go out and bring home a nice miyagé. If we saw an article in the newspaper mentioning a good play by Danjuro at the Kabukiza Theater, he would urge me to go, and would say that I could tell him all about it and consider that a miyagé. But he always would add, "You return at ten or eleven. Until then you are out and this is not my home. How lonesome it is! However, I shall be patient and wait for your interesting tale."

During his latter years he spoke of poor health; he depended on me, was devoted to me like a baby to its mother, and would wait for my return. When he heard my footstep, he would say jokingly, but with great delight, "Is that you, Mamma-san?" Should I be a bit late, he would worry, thinking that the *kuruma* had tipped over, or that some other misfortune had befallen me.

When he wished to hire a *kurumaya*, his first question was, "Does he love his wife ?" And if my answer were in the affirmative, he would say, "That is all right!" There was one person whom Hearn held in high esteem, but was greatly worried because he had such a stern expression toward his wife.

Just before Hearn's death a famous personage asked for an interview. There was, however, a man of the same name in England who had the reputation of abusing women, and Hearn thought that this person might be the one, and intended to refuse the request. Then he discovered that it was some one else and decided to meet him, but died before the interview. He became so angry with any one who abused the weak — women or children. I cannot mention them here individually, but there were many people who were once very intimate with Hearn and from whom he afterward became estranged because of these same reasons.

Hearn was provoked when he heard about any Japanese who had deserted his wife, or anything of that kind.

Hearn would have done anything for us, his wife and children. He did worry almost pitiably about things; for instance, about his naturalization and about employment for which he did not care.

He hated such innovations as electric cars. There were many occasions on which we could have had a telephone installed, but he would never listen to that proposition. He chose rather to have more servants than a telephone. At that time there was no electric nor gas light, but I don't think that he would have used them even if we had had them. He did not take a single ride on an electric car, and told us not to ride.

He objected to ride in the railway train when we were going to Yakizu. He wished to ride in a *kuruma* when he was tired of walking, but it was only necessary for him to be patient for seven hours, so we took the train. He thought how wonderful it would be if every one walked and there were no such things as trains. He liked to travel on boats; he said that he would enjoy the trip to Yakizu if he could go by boat.

When Hearn was coming to Japan, there was a great storm during the voyage. Everything on deck was washed away; the excitement was intense; even the sailors were seasick; he was the only one who felt as usual and asked for meals, and that astonished the people on the boat.

One time he came back from a walk and told me this story delightfully. "While passing through a part of Sendagaya, a student came and asked me in broken English: 'You, from where?' so I answered, 'Okubo.' 'Your country, which?' and I said, 'Japan.' The student asked again, 'You, what nationality?' and I replied, 'Japanese.' The student did not say another word, and looked at me curiously. He followed me. I was quiet, and walked on. And that student came as far as my gate, discovered the name on the gate, and then exclaimed, 'Hah! Koizumi Yakumo! Koizumi Yakumo !'" (Hearn's Japanese name.) That incident amused Hearn.

Hearn told another story. "One day, while in America, a stranger came to me

and borrowed a book. I did not get his
name, nor did he take my name. About a
year later he returned the book to me, invited me to a large restaurant, and gave
me a very good dinner. But even now I do
not know who it was."

IV

In the 37th year of Meiji, September 19, at three o'clock in the afternoon, I went to his study. He was walking round, putting his hands on his breast.

"Are you not well?" I asked.

"I have a new kind of sickness."

I inquired, "What kind?"

"Sickness of heart, I think."

"I think that you worry too much. You had better rest quietly."

This was my word of consolation for him.

Immediately I sent a two-man jinriki-sha for Dr. Kizawa, our family physician.

Hearn never wished to have me or the children see him troubled. He told me that I had better go away and not worry; but I was worried, and I stayed there near his desk. He started to write something, and I advised him to keep quiet.

Hearn asked me to leave him alone, and finished his writing. He said, "This is a letter to Ume-san. If trouble comes, he will help you. Perhaps, if this pain of mine increases, I may die. If I die, do not weep. Buy a little urn; you can find one for three or four sen. Put my bones in it, and bury it near a quiet temple in the country. I shall not like it if you cry. Amuse the children and play cards with them — how much better I shall enjoy that! There will be no need of announcing my death. If any one asks, reply, 'Oh, he died some time ago!' That will be quite proper."

I asked him not to talk so sadly. When I said that to him, he replied, "I am very serious. Honestly, from my heart," he said, emphatically. Then he added, "No use," and rested quietly.

Several minutes later he stood up and said, "I have no more pain. I wish to take a bath." He wanted a cold bath, and took one in the bathroom.

"The pain has gone entirely. Strange — I feel very well. Mamma-san, the sickness has left me," he said. "How about a little whiskey for me?"

I thought to myself, "Whiskey is not good for the heart"; but he insisted.

I said, "I don't know. However, if you wish some badly, I will give you some with water."

I gave him a glass, and he raised the glass to his lips and said, "I shall not die."

It made me feel better. Then he told me that he had had this particular pain for several days. "I will rest a little while," he said, and got on to the bed with a book.

In the mean time the doctor had come. Hearn said, "What shall I do?" He left his book and went into the guest-room, where he received the doctor. He said, laughingly, "You must excuse me, my sickness is gone."

After the doctor had examined him, he told us that there was nothing serious the matter, and, as usual, talked and joked.

Hearn was almost always in good health. He dreaded like a child to have a doctor examine him, or to take medicine. He would not have a doctor unless I begged him to. When he was a trifle ill, and I failed to get a doctor in time, he would say to me afterwards, "I am greatly pleased that you forgot the doctor."

Hearn, when he was not writing, would walk around the room, or up and down the *roka*, thinking things. Even when he was sick, he was not the kind of man who could stay in bed.

Two or three days before he died, Osaki, the maid, told me that the cherry tree was blossoming out of season (*kaer-izaki*) in the garden by the studio. (In my household things like that are of great interest. To-day some little bamboo-sprouts have shot up in the woods; look! a yellow butterfly is flitting about; Kazuo, my son, found a little ant-hill; a toad came to the door; or the sunset is full of beautifully changing colors.) Such details as these drew more attention from us than if they had been important matters, and Hearn was informed of every one of these incidents. He was delighted to hear about them. It seems funny that this gave us so much pleasure. Toads, butterflies, ants, spiders, cicadas, bamboo-sprouts, and sunsets were among Papa-san's best friends.

Now, in Japan, *kaerizaki* (to have the cherry tree blossom out of season) is not a sign of good fortune, so it worried me a little. But when I told Hearn about it, he was delighted, and replied, *"Arigato"* (Thanks). He went near the edge of the *roka*, or narrow veranda that runs around the outside of our house, and, looking at the flowers, said, "Hello." He added, "'It is warm like spring,' the cherry tree thought. 'Ah! this is my world again'; and blossomed."

Meditating a little while, he said again, "Pity! soon it will become cold and frightened, and die."

The flowers bloomed just one day, on the 27th; in the evening all the petals had fluttered to the ground. This cherry tree blossomed every season, and Hearn loved it. Probably the cherry tree remembered that, and blossomed to bid him farewell.

Hearn used to get up early in the morning; but as he feared to disturb our dreams, he always waited in his studio, sitting by the *hibachi* (bronze bowl of lighted charcoal) and smoking quietly.

He preferred a long kind of pipe. He had about a hundred of them. The oldest one he had the year he came, and the others had been added. Each pipe was carved. Among the carvings were: Urashima (the Rip van Winkle of Japan); the *kinuta* of autumnal nights (the *kinuta* is a wooden mallet used by women to pound linen); eggplants; praying demons; crows on a leafless branch; utensils of the tea-ceremony; and verses of poems, for instance, "To-night of last year." These were the favorite ones among the hundred.

It seems that it was interesting to him to smoke these. He chose one from many, and always looked first at the mouthpiece and the bowl, then lighted it. Sitting on the floor-cushion very correctly, he rocked himself slowly back and forth, and smoked.

The day he died, the morning of the 26th, about half-past six, I went to his study. He was already up and smoking. I greeted him: "Good-morning!"

He seemed to be thinking about something. Then he said, "I had a very unusual dream last night."

We always talked about our dreams. I inquired what kind of a dream it was.

He replied, "I traveled for a very long distance. Now that I am smoking here, it hardly seems to have been a real journey. It was like a dream," he continued; "not a journey in Europe, nor in Japan — it was a strange place." He seemed to be enjoying himself.

Before they went to bed, it was the custom for our three children to say, "Papa-san, good-night, pleasant dreams." And their Papa-san replied, " The same to you." Or, in Japanese, *"Yoki yume mimasho."*

That morning Kazuo, my son, before going to school, came and said, "Good-morning." To this greeting his Papa-san replied, "Pleasant dreams." "The same to you," said Kazuo.

At eleven o'clock in the morning he was walking up and down the *roka*. He saw a *kakemono* (painting) depicting the sun-rise, in the library *tokonoma* (raised recess at one end of a room). This is a picture of early morning. Many crows are flying around, and it looks like a scene from a dream. Hearn made the remark: "What beautiful scenery! I should like to live in a place like that."

He bought many *kakemono*. He did not decide to hang this one or that one, but left the choice to me. He enjoyed looking at whichever one I hung. He looked at it as a visitor would, and was pleased. He had a very aesthetic taste, I think. He liked tea and drank it with pleasure. When I made tea he played the part of a guest. He did not perform the intricate details, but he understood the principle of the *cha-no-yu*, or tea-ceremony.

Hearn enjoyed listening to singing insects. That autumn we had a *matsu-mushi* (insects like crickets). Toward the end of September, when the song of insects is hushed, it made us all feel sad to hear the *matsu-mushi*.

I asked Hearn, "Do you hear that noise?"

He replied, "That poor little insect has sung for us beautifully. How much I enjoyed it! As the weather grows colder and colder, does it know that it will have to die soon? Poor, sad little insect!" After saying that, so piteously, he continued, "Some of these warm days we had better let it go into the bushes."

The early blossoming of the cherry tree, the dream of a long journey, and the dying song of the *matsu-mushi* must have been signs of his death, of which it makes me very, very sad to think, even to-day.

In the afternoon he asked, "What book shall we send to Fujizaki-san, who is in the Manchurian campaign?" He looked for the book on the library shelves, and afterwards wrote a letter to his friend.

While he was eating supper he looked unusually happy, and joked and laughed loudly. "Papa-san, good Papa-san!" — "Sweet chickens!" — He talked with the children, and, as usual, walked round the library *roka*.

In a little less than an hour he came back to me with a drawn face, and said quietly, "Mamma-san, the sickness of the other day has come back again."

I went with him. For a little while he walked around the room with his hands on his breast. I advised him to lie quietly on the bed, and he did so. Very soon after that he was no longer of this world.

He died without any pain, having a little smile around his mouth. It could not be helped, if it was the order of Heaven. I wish that I could have taken care of him, and given all my strength in nursing him. This was too easy a death for me.[1]

[1] A literal translation, which means that Mrs. Hearn regretted having been given no opportunity to show her love and devotion before death. — THE TRANSLATOR.

V

I may name again some things that
Hearn liked extremely: the west, sunsets,
summer, the sea, swimming, banana trees,
cryptomerias (the *sugi*, the Japanese cedar), lonely cemeteries, insects, "Kwaidan"
(ghostly tales), Urashima, and *Horai*
(songs) . The places he liked were: Mar-
tinique, Matsué, Miho-no-seki, Higosaki,
and Yakizu. He was fond of beefsteak and
plum-pudding, and enjoyed smoking. He
disliked liars, abuse of the weak, Prince
Albert coats, white shirts, the City of New
York, and many other things. One of his
pleasures was to wear the *yukata* in his
study and listen quietly to the voice of the
locust.

We often took walks together, crossing
the bridge of Ochiai to the neighborhood of
Arai-no-yakushi. Every time that Hearn
saw the chimney of the Ochiai crematory,
he would think, as he said, that he himself
would soon come out as smoke from that
chimney. He always liked quiet temple
grounds. Had there been a temple, a very
small and dilapidated building with walls
overgrown with weeds, it would have been

an ideal resting-place for Hearn's body.
But such a place was hard to find quickly.
His wish was to have a small tombstone
invisible from the outside he always spoke
of that. But it was finally decided that the
service should be held at the Kobudera
temple, and he was buried in the cemetery of Zoshigaya.

As previously mentioned, Hearn had
lost interest in the Kobudera temple, but
there were many ties from former days.
More recently we had associated with the
abbot of the temple Denbo-in, in Asakusa.
We asked the abbot to officiate, and then
the services were held at Kobudera. Hearn
was interested in the Zen sect.

The Zen sect, founded by Dharma
(Daruma) in India, in A.D. 513, and
brought by him to China, was introduced
thence into Japan by the bonze Dosho, in
the seventh century. Rejected at first, it
was revived in 1192 by the bonze Eisei,
who is regarded as its founder in Nippon.
It is sometimes called the "sect of contemplation," and its doctrines, as interpreted
by the many scholarly men who adopted
them, have made, perhaps, the greatest

impression of any of the sects on the national thought and life. Its teachings are based upon the principle that every one may arrive at the knowledge of the law and nature of Buddha by meditation, without being influenced by dissenting beliefs. Perchance because its adoption by the Japanese was coeval with the establishment of military feudalism, its dogmas found special favor among the *samurai* of old Japan, since their tendency was to render one indifferent to danger or death. The most powerful of its branches, the Sodo-shu, was founded by Dosen in 1227. Daruma is specially revered in the Zen temples, where he is portrayed as an unshaven (and somewhat ruffianly) ascetic, clad in a red robe and lost in deep meditation. According to tradition he sat for nine years in uninterrupted contemplation and remained so motionless that his legs rotted off. His image is a favorite one for toys and as a tobacconist's sign. Dosho is said to have been the first to introduce cremation into Japan.[1]

---

[1] Terry's *Japanese Empire,* page cxcix.

But the house of Koizumi was originally of the Jodo sect, so perhaps the temple Dentsu-in might have been preferable;
however, at that time the temple was not
kept up and I did not feel like going there.
The cemeteries in the temple grounds
were often removed, and I did not consider
it quite safe to bury him in such a place,
so we chose a public cemetery about which
we did not have to worry. The cemetery at
Aoyama was too modern, and Hearn never
liked it. We decided upon the public cemetery of Zoshigaya because it was quieter
and had a better location. Moreover, Zoshigaya was a place that Hearn used to like
to visit. Once he asked us to accompany
him to a fine place, and took me and the
children to Zoshigaya.

While taking walks around Kishibojin,
he often asked me how I liked the cawing
of the crows. The localities along the way
from Sekiguchi to Zoshigaya were excellent, and Hearn said that he wished he
were twenty years younger, he should so
like to build a house on the top of a certain
hill. It was too bad he could not.

He and I took a walk together to look
at gates in the neighborhood of Zoshigaya,
as we wished to alter our own front gate.
It was about two weeks before his death,
and it was the last walk that he and I were
to take together. The work of altering our
gate was begun two days before his death,
and after his death we hurried to have it
ready in time for the funeral.

THE END

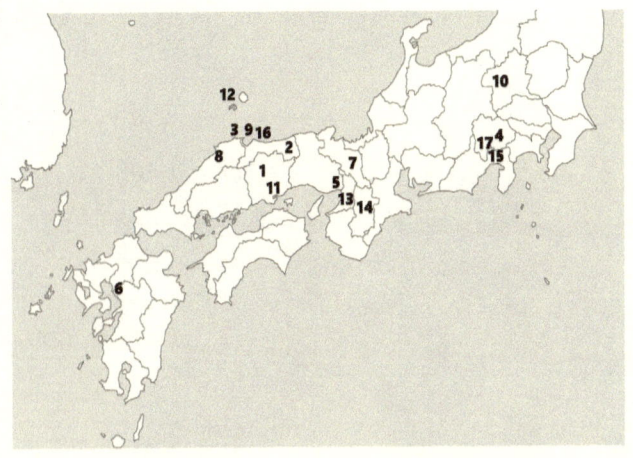

Places mentioned: